Hot Soup

by Charles Dillard   illustrated by Bernard Adnet

Harcourt

Orlando   Boston   Dallas   Chicago   San Diego

Visit *The Learning Site!*

www.harcourtschool.com

ISBN 0-15-325474-2

12 13 14 15 16 17 18 19 20   121   10 09 08 07 06 05

Ordering Options
ISBN 0-15-325468-8 (Collection)
ISBN 0-15-326552-3 (package of 5)

I have hot soup for you.

I like it in my cup.

I like it in my mug.

I like it in my pot.

I like it in my can.

I like it in my tub.

I can fill the tub.